INTERFACT

THE BOOK AND DISK **THAT WORK TOGETHER**

DINOSAURS

TM

CHANHASSEN, MINNESOTA · LONDON

Two-Can Publishing
An imprint of Creative Publishing international, Inc.
18705 Lake Drive East
Chanhassen, MN 55317
1-800-328-3895
www.two-canpublishing.com

Created by
act-two
346 Old Street
London
EC1V 9RB

Project Manager: Deborah Kespert
Art Director: Belinda Webster
Senior Designers: Liz Adcock, James Marks
Editors: Emma Johnson, Paul Virr
Author: Jen Green
Illustrators: Simone End (main illustrations), Peter Dennis (story)
Consultant: Mike Benton

ISBN 1-58728-343-3

Library of Congress Cataloging-in-Publication Data: pending

Photographic credits: front cover Science Photo Library/Roger Harris;
p.8-9 The Natural History Museum, London; p.12 OSF/Breck P. Kent;
p.13 Corbis/Jonathon Blair; p.14 Ardea/Francois Gottier; p.16 Ardea/Pat Morris;
p18 OSF/Frithjof Skibbe; p.22 OSF/E. R. Degginger/AA; p.27 Bruce Coleman

1 2 3 4 5 6 08 07 06 05 04 03

Printed in Hong Kong

INTERFACT™

THE BOOK AND DISK ▼ THAT WORK TOGETHER

INTERFACT will have you hooked in minutes – and that's a fact!

🟡 The disk is packed with interactive games, puzzles, quizzes, and activities that are challenging, fun, and full of interesting facts.

▶ Play BONE ZONE to learn about the parts that make up a dinosaur.

🔵 Open the book and discover more fascinating information, highlighted with colorful illustrations and photographs.

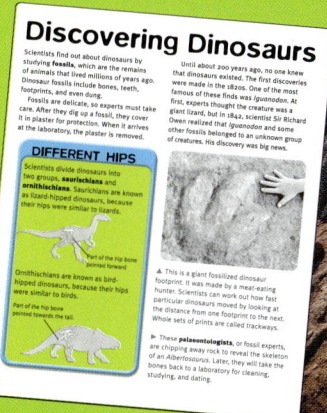

◀ Find out about fossil experts and their amazing discoveries.

🟣 To make the most of INTERFACT, use the book and disk together. Look out for special signs called Disk Links and Bookmarks. To find out more, turn to page 43.

40

BOOKMARK

DISK LINK
In BONE ZONE, piece together a dinosaur skeleton, then watch it come to life!

DISK LINK

Once you've clicked on to INTERFACT, you'll never look back.

LOAD UP!
Go to **page 41** to find out how to load your disk and click into action.

What's on the Disk?

? Help Screen

Learn how to use your Interfact disk in no time at all. Use the speaker button to switch the sound on or off. Use your arrow keys to select a game or bring up the Help icon.

Welcome to

INTERFACT

Dinosaurs

To have a look at all the different things on the disk, simply click the arrow keys with your mouse.

As you do this, you'll see a description of each activity in the reading box.

Click on the picture at the top of the screen to select the activity you want to investigate.

Click on the speaker if you'd like to hear the text read out. Just click on the speaker again to switch it off.

And remember! Any words in blue and underlined like this are hot. Touch them with your mouse for more information.

VOICE ON

Ah, hello! I've been expecting you. Are you ready to help me with my latest dinosaur discovery?

Bone Zone

Prove that you're a fossil expert by helping the professor to build a dinosaur. Work out how the bones fit together, then put them into place!

Extinction

Travel back in time to the world of the dinosaurs in this exciting quiz game. Answer the questions correctly, and you'll win a fantastic surprise. Get them wrong, and you'll end up as lunch!

It's a dinosaur egg...and it looks like it's about to hatch!

Dinos in Disguise

Use the clues to identify the mystery dinosaur that's hiding in the cave. You have three tries to get it right. If you know your dinosaurs, you're sure to pick up the points.

Spinosaurus
Ankylosaurus
Parasaurolophus
Torosaurus

0 10 30 50

Survival

You'll need a steady hand to guide the baby *Maiasaura* back to the safety of the nesting ground. Munch on tasty snacks along the way and dodge a hungry *Tyrannosaurus*. Arrive back home safely, and you can find out lots of fascinating dinosaur facts.

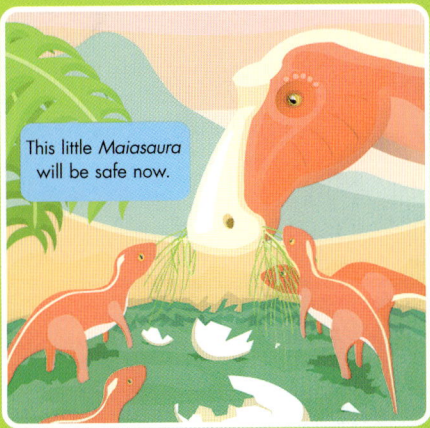

This little *Maiasaura* will be safe now.

Dino Doubles

Match up the dinosaur pictures to their names. Be quick, though – you need to pick the pairs before the timer runs out!

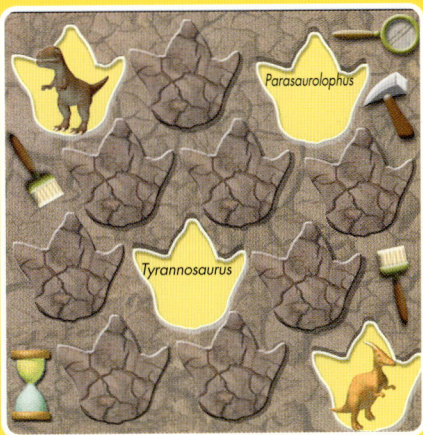

Parasaurolophus

Tyrannosaurus

What's in the Book?

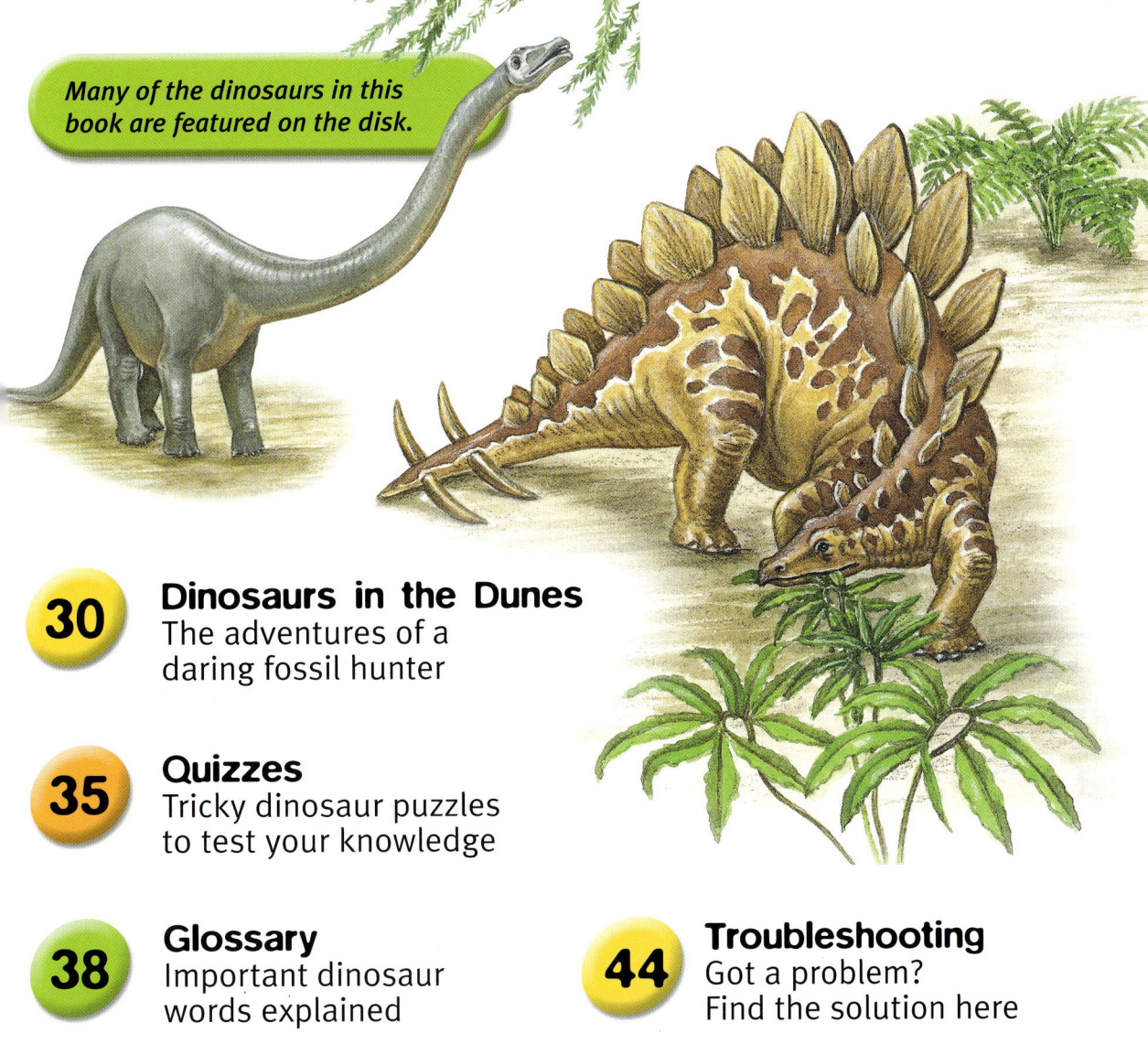

Many of the dinosaurs in this book are featured on the disk.

*All words in the text that appear in **bold**
can be found in the glossary.*

Looking at Dinosaurs

About 250 million years ago, a group of amazing animals called dinosaurs appeared on Earth. For the next 185 million years, they ruled the planet.

Dinosaurs were ancient **reptiles**. Like modern-day reptiles, they had scaly skin and laid eggs. Some were as small as chickens, while others were as big as jumbo jets! Long before humans existed, the dinosaurs mysteriously died out. No one knows for sure why this happened.

DID YOU KNOW?

● The remains of about 800 different kinds of dinosaur have been discovered.

● One recent discovery is named *Sinosauropteryx*. Experts believe it had a feather-like covering on its skin.

● The name *dinosaur* comes from the ancient Greek words *deinos* and *sauros,* which together mean "terrible lizard."

▶ You can see life-size models of many dinosaurs in museums. Experts study dinosaur remains to figure out how big and what shape the models should be.

DISK LINK
Play DINO DOUBLES to see if you can beat the clock and match all the dinosaurs to their names!

When Dinosaurs Ruled

Dinosaurs lived during a time called the **Mesozoic era**. The world was a much warmer place than it is now, and there were no ice caps at the **poles**. Dinosaurs shared the land with small **mammals**, insects, birds, and other reptiles.

The dinosaurs adapted well to their surroundings and soon **evolved** to become stronger than other creatures. The first dinosaurs were all meat eaters. Their legs were tucked under their bodies, which allowed them to run fast when hunting.

LIVING ON LAND

When dinosaurs first appeared, all the land on Earth was joined together in one huge **continent** called Pangaea. Today, there are seven separate continents.

The world in the time of the dinosaurs

N
Pangaea
W Equator E
S

The world today

North America
N
Europe
Asia
Africa
W Equator E
South America
Australia
Antarctica
S

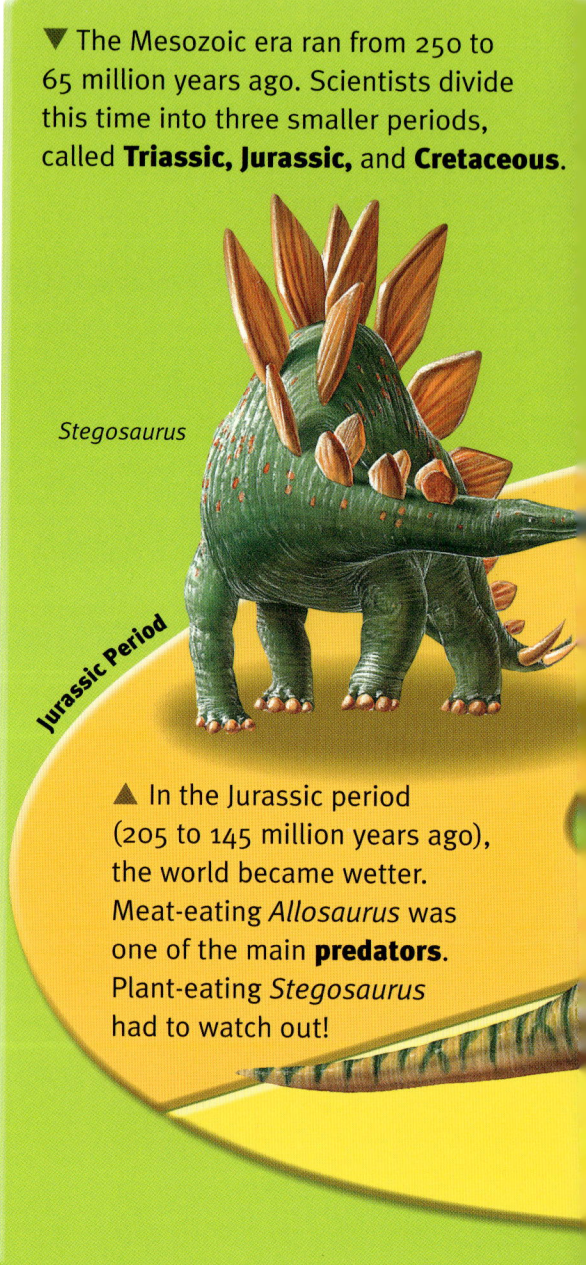

▼ The Mesozoic era ran from 250 to 65 million years ago. Scientists divide this time into three smaller periods, called **Triassic, Jurassic,** and **Cretaceous**.

Stegosaurus

Jurassic Period

▲ In the Jurassic period (205 to 145 million years ago), the world became wetter. Meat-eating *Allosaurus* was one of the main **predators**. Plant-eating *Stegosaurus* had to watch out!

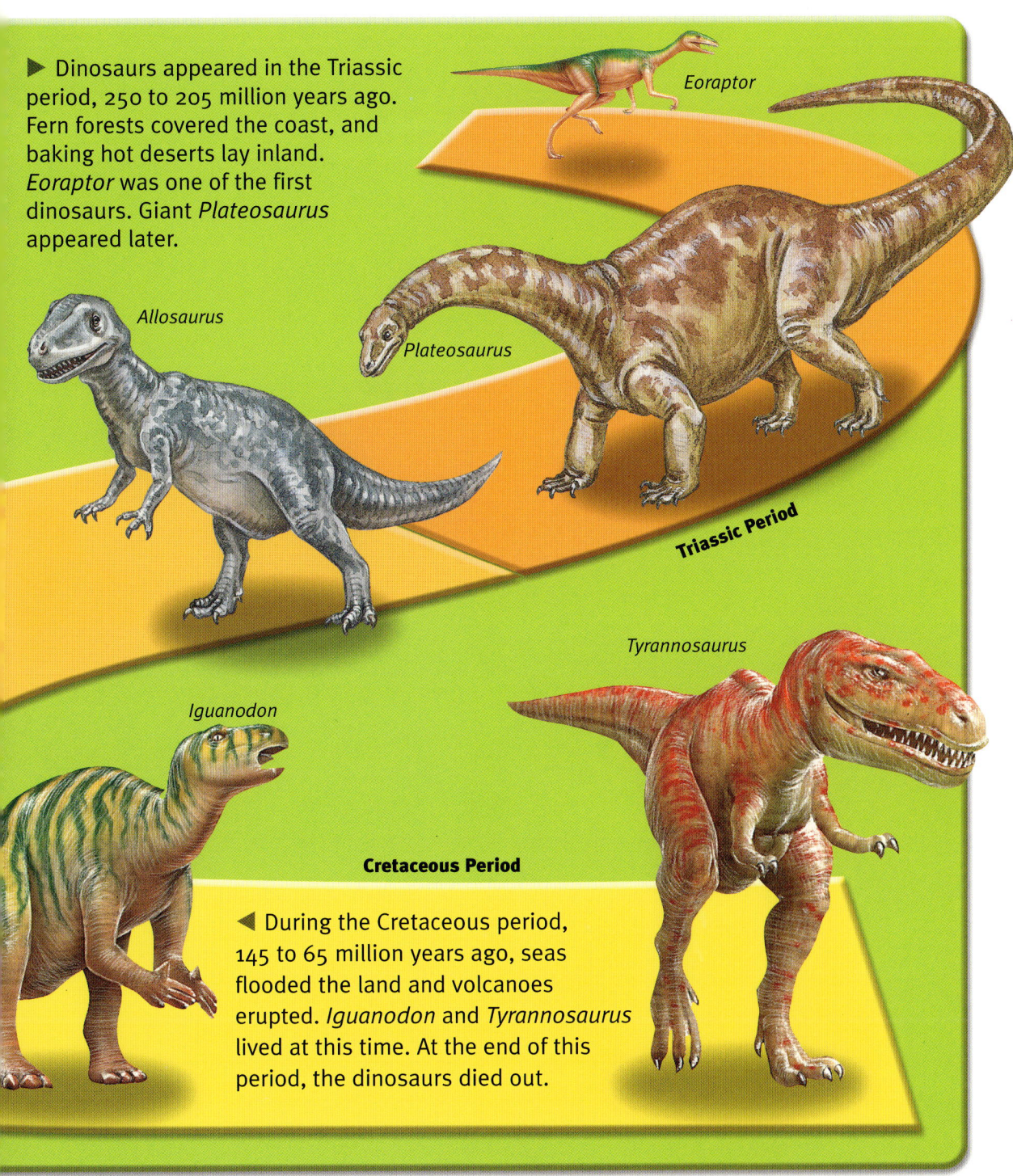

▶ Dinosaurs appeared in the Triassic period, 250 to 205 million years ago. Fern forests covered the coast, and baking hot deserts lay inland. *Eoraptor* was one of the first dinosaurs. Giant *Plateosaurus* appeared later.

Eoraptor

Allosaurus

Plateosaurus

Triassic Period

Tyrannosaurus

Iguanodon

Cretaceous Period

◀ During the Cretaceous period, 145 to 65 million years ago, seas flooded the land and volcanoes erupted. *Iguanodon* and *Tyrannosaurus* lived at this time. At the end of this period, the dinosaurs died out.

Discovering Dinosaurs

Scientists find out about dinosaurs by studying **fossils**, which are the remains of animals that lived millions of years ago. Dinosaur fossils include bones, teeth, footprints, and even dung.

Fossils are delicate, so experts must take care. After they dig up a fossil, they cover it in plaster for protection. When it arrives at the laboratory, the plaster is removed.

Until about 200 years ago, no one knew that dinosaurs existed. The first discoveries were made in the 1820s. One of the most famous of these finds was *Iguanodon*. At first, experts thought the creature was a giant lizard, but in 1842, scientist Sir Richard Owen realized that *Iguanodon* and some other fossils belonged to an unknown group of creatures. His discovery was big news.

DIFFERENT HIPS

Scientists divide dinosaurs into two groups, **saurischians** and **ornithischians**. Saurichians are known as lizard-hipped dinosaurs, because their hips were similar to those of lizards.

Part of the hip bone pointed forward.

Ornithischians are known as bird-hipped dinosaurs, because their hips were similar to those of birds.

Part of the hip bone pointed towards the tail.

▲ This is a giant fossilized dinosaur footprint. It was made by a meat-eating hunter. Scientists can work out how fast particular dinosaurs moved by looking at the distance from one footprint to the next. Whole sets of prints are called trackways.

▶ These **palaeontologists**, or fossil experts, are chipping away rock to reveal the skeleton of an *Albertosaurus*. Later, they will take the bones back to a laboratory for cleaning, studying, and dating.

DISK LINK

Help the professor piece together the bones of a giant dinosaur when you play BONE ZONE.

Meat-Eating Hunters

The most ferocious dinosaurs were the meat eaters, or **carnivores**. They included *Tyrannosaurus, Allosaurus,* and *Velociraptor.* Meat eaters belonged to a group of dinosaurs called **theropods**. Theropods all ran on two legs, had three-toed feet, and had sharp, curved teeth.

Large meat eaters such as *Tyrannosaurus* mainly hunted other dinosaurs. These fierce predators had huge heads with strong jaws. One look at these giants, and other creatures fled for their lives! Smaller meat-eating dinosaurs chased after smaller prey, such as **mammals,** lizards, birds, fish, and frogs.

DISK LINK
In EXTINCTION, answer the dinosaur questions correctly or the fossil hunter will soon end up as lunch!

▲ This huge tooth of a *Tyrannosaurus* is almost twice the length of an adult's hand. The dinosaur had up to 60 teeth in its mouth. Each one curved backwards, giving it a firm grip on any animal trapped in its jaws.

▼ *Tyrannosaurus* was too large and heavy to chase its **prey** for long. Instead, it probably hid and waited for a victim, such as a *Nodosaurus*, to come along. Then it charged at the creature and tore away huge chunks of flesh.

Weapons of Attack

Meat-eating dinosaurs used their sharp teeth and long claws to kill prey. Giants such as *Tyrannosaurus* and *Albertosaurus* relied on their strength to keep hold of food. Smaller meat eaters often had extra weapons on their bodies to help.

Deinonychus, whose name means "terrible claw," grabbed and slashed at its prey with the extra-long claws on each back foot. *Baryonyx* speared fish with the huge hooks on its hands. The smaller meat eaters could run fast, too.

All meat eaters made good use of their senses when tracking animals. Many of them could see, hear, and smell well. Some also used their quick wits to plan their attacks. Small dinosaurs mostly hunted together. They circled their victims first, then quickly attacked from all sides.

▶ *Deinonychus* may have hunted in packs to bring down victims too large for a single dinosaur to kill. Here you can see four *Deinonychus* ripping into the flesh of a plant-eating *Tenontosaurus*.

▲ Few creatures could escape the fearsome bite and huge jaws of an *Allosaurus*. Its jaws had extra hinges, just as a modern-day snake's jaws do. This allowed *Allosaurus* to open its mouth very wide and bite off huge chunks of flesh.

SWIFT HUNTERS

Velociraptors were speedy, medium-sized hunters that lived during the Cretaceous period. They got their name, which means "swift thief," because experts think they stole other dinosaurs' eggs to eat.

Plant Munchers

Not all dinosaurs were blood-thirsty hunters. Most were gentle plant-eaters, or **herbivores.** One of the most amazing groups was the giant, long-necked **sauropod** group. These graceful beasts included *Diplodocus*, *Apatosaurus,* and *Brachiosaurus*. They were some of the tallest animals that have ever lived on our planet.

The sauropods reached into treetops with their long necks to pluck fruit and leaves. Shorter plant eaters, such as horned *Triceratops*, spiky *Ankylosaurus,* and plated *Stegosaurus*, grazed on lower growing bushes. Plant eaters spent the whole day munching to fill their bellies.

▲ In Triassic times, plant-eating dinosaurs feasted on horsetail ferns like the ones above. Palm-like cycads and **conifers** grew in the Jurassic period. Flowers, such as magnolia, grew in Cretaceous times.

BEAKS AND HANDS

Plant-eating dinosaurs had jaws and teeth suited to their diet. A few also had nimble hands to help them pick their food from trees and bushes.

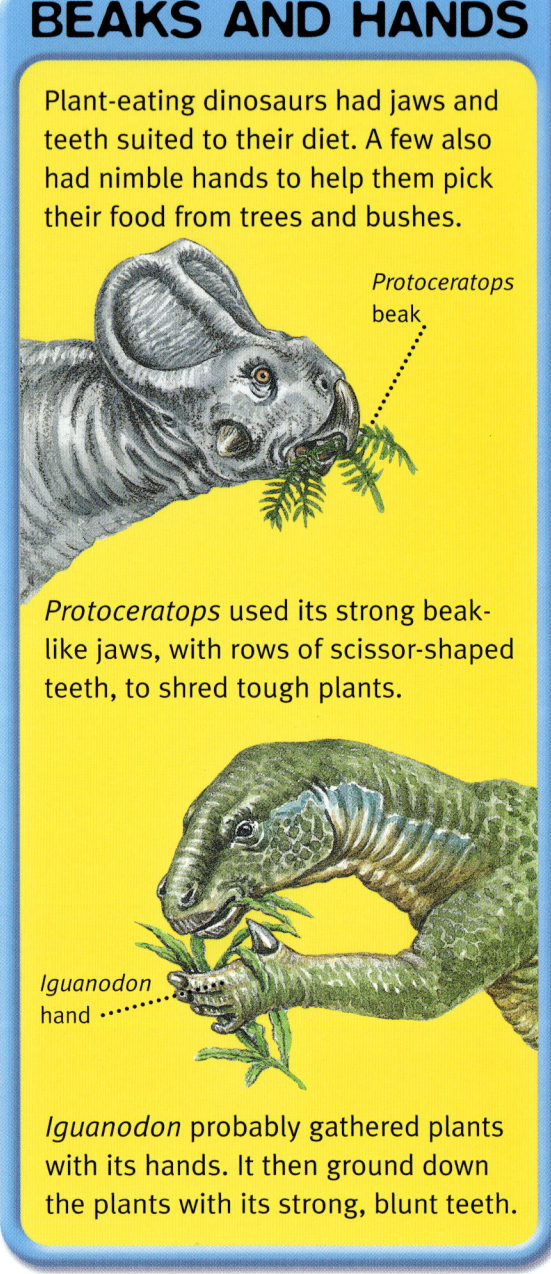

Protoceratops beak

Protoceratops used its strong beak-like jaws, with rows of scissor-shaped teeth, to shred tough plants.

Iguanodon hand

Iguanodon probably gathered plants with its hands. It then ground down the plants with its strong, blunt teeth.

▼ Long-necked *Diplodocus* raked leaves into its mouth with its teeth. It could not chew, so it swallowed its food whole. It also swallowed stones, which churned the food in its stomach into a pulp.

▶ *Stegosaurus* munched leaves with its broad teeth. This massive creature was 30 feet (9 m) long but had a small mouth and a brain the size of a walnut!

DISK LINK
Listen to the clues to bring the mystery dinosaur out of the dark when you play DINOS IN DISGUISE.

Dinosaur Defenses

Large meat eaters were always on the lookout for plant eaters to surprise and attack. But plant eaters had many ways of defending themselves.

Tall *Diplodocus* could spot danger from far away. Bulky *Triceratops* gathered in small herds for protection. Smaller dinosaurs, such as long-legged *Struthiomimus*, usually got out of trouble by making a quick getaway.

▶ *Triceratops* was a giant plant eater. It was built like a rhino and had a bony neck frill and three horns on its head. It put up a good fight against the fierce *Tyrannosaurus*.

Several dinosaurs also had body armor for extra protection. Rows of bony plates stuck up along the back of *Stegosaurus*. *Ankylosaurus* was covered from head to tail with bony plates and spikes. One dinosaur, called *Minmi*, even had plates covering part of its belly. There was a drawback to armor, though. It made these dinosaurs move more slowly.

ON THE DEFENSIVE

Many dinosaurs used their tails to fight off attackers.

Euoplocephalus

Euoplocephalus had a bony club on its tail, heavy enough to smash another creature's leg.

Stegosaurus

The sharp spikes on a *Stegosaurus's* tail could slit the belly of an attacker.

Apatosaurus

Apatosaurus's tail narrowed to a bony rod. The dinosaur lashed its tail like a whip to fight off enemies.

Dinosaur Babies

Dinosaurs gave birth to their young by laying eggs. After mating, females laid from two to thirty eggs in nests on the ground. Some built nests as big as 6 feet (2 m) wide. Like birds today, dinosaurs may have sat on their eggs to keep them warm until the babies hatched. They laid small eggs for such huge creatures. None was bigger than a soccer ball. If the eggs grew much bigger, the shells would have been too thick for the hatchlings to crack open.

Some newly hatched dinosaurs were strong enough to fend for themselves.

Others needed weeks of care. The young of a few kinds of dinosaur stayed in family groups until they were almost fully grown. Dinosaur family groups moved around together in search of food. Fossil footprints show that young dinosaurs traveled in the center of the group for safety.

DISK LINK
Play SURVIVAL to see if you can guide the baby dinosaur to its nest. Watch out for the dangers on the way.

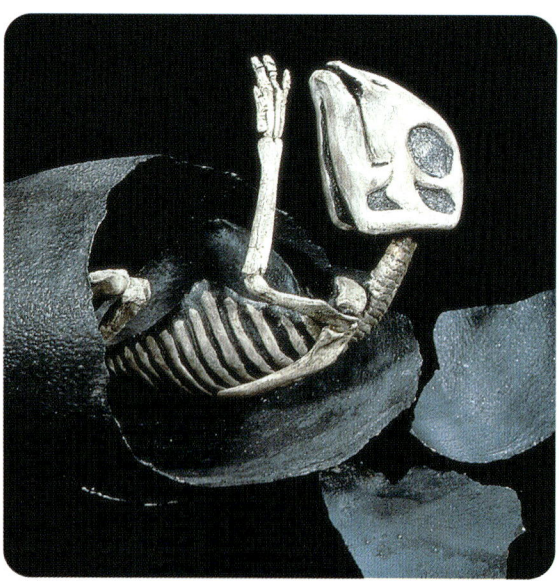

▲ This amazing **fossil** of a baby *Maiasaura*, about to hatch from its shell, was found in Montana. This dinosaur baby was so small it could easily sit in your hands. Yet as an adult, it could be as long as a bus.

▼ *Maiasaura* dinosaurs nested in large groups called colonies so that many adults could watch over the babies. Mothers, and possibly fathers and older brothers and sisters, brought food to the little ones until they were strong enough to leave the nest.

Land, Sea, and Sky

During the time of the dinosaurs, many other kinds of animal also lived on Earth. Swamps and forests were home to insects, froglike **amphibians**, birds, and mammals. Crocodiles, lizards, and other reptiles crawled across the land or swam in lakes and oceans. A few of these creatures looked like dinosaurs, but they were only distant relatives.

Mighty reptiles, such as long-necked plesiosaurs and long-nosed ichthyosaurs, ruled the oceans. These creatures were the ocean killers of the dinosaur age, spending their days hunting fish and squid.

Flying reptiles called pterosaurs shared the skies with birds. Some pterosaurs were as big as hang gliders, and others were as small as crows.

▼ During the Cretaceous period, you could spot all kinds of amazing creatures swimming in the sea, flying in the skies, or scuttling through the trees.

▲ This small, mouselike mammal is called *Alphadon*. It lived in the trees, probably gripping the branches with its bendy toes and curly tail. *Alphadon* fed on fruit, insects, and any other small animals it could catch.

◀ Pterosaurs, such as this *Pteranodon,* had huge wings covered with thin, stretchy skin. They flew low in the sky, diving to the surface of the water to scoop up fish in their enormous beaks.

◀ Plesiosaurs, such as this *Elasmosaurus,* had long necks to snap up fish. A plesiosaur paddled along with its four flippers, raising its head out of the water now and then to breathe.

▼ Ichthyosaurs, such as this *Opthalmosaurus,* looked like fish, with bodies shaped like a dolphin's. An ichthyosaur's powerful tail helped it to move swiftly through the water. It used its long flippers to steer.

End of the Dinosaurs

At the end of the Cretaceous period, 65 million years ago, all the dinosaurs mysteriously died out.

Some scientists think that a **meteorite** from space crashed to Earth, creating a giant cloud of dust that blocked the sunlight. Plants withered and food was hard to find, so the dinosaurs died. Other experts think that ash and poisonous gases from giant volcanoes brought about the dinosaurs' end.

▶ Dinosaurs such as duck-billed *Parasaurolophus* and club-tailed *Ankylosaurus* may have watched in terror as a giant meteorite hit the Earth. The effect would have been similar to a huge explosion.

Even though dinosaurs disappeared, many small mammals, including tiny *Alphadon*, did not. Flying pterosaurs died out, and so did the magnificent swimming reptiles. But birds, fish, snakes, lizards, turtles, and crocodiles all survived. These kinds of animals are still with us today.

DID YOU KNOW?

● In 1990, a huge crater was found off the coast of Mexico. It was caused by a meteorite hitting Earth. Scientists think the crater was formed 65 million years ago, at the time when the dinosaurs died out.

● There are all kinds of explanations for the death of the dinosaurs. One of the oddest is that they grew so big they fell over, then couldn't get up again to find food!

▲ This is a fossil of the first bird, *Archaeopteryx*. It had feathers and wings like a bird, but the teeth and claws of a dinosaur. The discovery has led some scientists to believe that birds evolved from dinosaurs.

Dinosaur Champions

Who are the dinosaur champions? The largest, the tallest, the fastest, and the smallest? It is not always easy to decide which dinosaur should take the trophy. Also, as experts discover and study new fossils, the champions may change.

One thing is certain though – dinosaurs were more powerful than any other creatures that ever walked the earth. They had few enemies to fear, and most of them made even the largest animals alive today look small.

▼ *Compsognathus*
Meat eater
Late Jurassic

Compsognathus was the tiniest dinosaur. It was about 3 feet (1 m) long from head to tail, with a body the size of a turkey. This speedy hunter chased insects and lizards for its dinner.

▶ *Gallimimus*
Meat and plant eater
Late Cretaceous

Gallimimus, shown on the right, and its relative *Ornithomimus* were in competition for the fastest dinosaurs. They had short bodies and strong back legs for running quickly. Experts think they raced along at about 34 miles per hour (55 km per hour), about the same pace as a greyhound.

▼ *Diplodocus*
Plant eater
Late Jurassic

Diplodocus was one of the largest dinosaurs. It measured at least 72 feet (22 m) from head to tail and was longer than two buses! However, there is competition from another sauropod, *Argentinosaurus*, which may have been even larger.

▲ *Brachiosaurus*
Plant eater
Late Jurassic

Brachiosaurus was one of the tallest dinosaurs. It stood over 50 feet (16 m) tall, and its tail was as long as a tennis court! Amazingly, a recent discovery named *Sauroposeidon* may have been even taller.

Dinosaurs in the Dunes

Roy Chapman Andrews was an American explorer with a passion for dinosaurs. During the 1920s, he led many daring expeditions to Outer Mongolia, in Asia, to hunt for dinosaur fossils and fame. This is the imagined diary of his adventures.

February 1920

Today I met with Henry Fairfield Osborn, the president of the American Museum of Natural History where I work. I see him often, but today was different. We talked about dinosaurs, and he has given me a fantastic idea – to set up a fossil-hunting expedition. Both of us are convinced that the first dinosaurs came from Outer Mongolia, in central Asia. I'm sure there are hundreds of fossils out there waiting to be discovered, and I'm the person to find them! I must start work immediately and find a team of experts. This is the chance I've been waiting for to make my name. But it could be a dangerous trip.

April 1922

After months of careful preparation, we've finally reached the Gobi Desert, in Mongolia. This must surely be one of the most desolate places on earth. There is nothing but rock, scrub, and sand as far as the eye can see. By day, the sun bears down and it is boiling hot, but the nights are freezing cold. We are ready for the fossil-hunting to begin.

May 1922

Our convoy of three cars, two trucks, and 75 camels has been winding through this scorching desert for weeks now. So far we've found nothing. Today, a terrible sandstorm forced us to a halt. Everyone is keen to move on as soon as the winds die down.

June 1922

We are deep in the heart of the Gobi Desert. The heat is incredible. Poisonous snakes and scorpions lurk amongst the rocks. I've told the team to be extremely careful when they are digging for fossils.

We must also take care to avoid the Chinese and Russian soldiers who are fighting over this area. We are well armed, but I have mounted a machine gun on the car leading the convoy for extra protection.

July 1922

We have made an amazing find! While walking along a dried-up riverbed, one of the drivers discovered a huge fossilized jawbone. We explored the surrounding area and managed to recover almost all of the skeleton to which it belongs. I think this ancient animal was a type of giant rhinoceros. It's bigger than one of our trucks! We've named it *Baluchitherium*. Our first trip has ended in triumph. We've packed the fossils into crates and are returning to China.

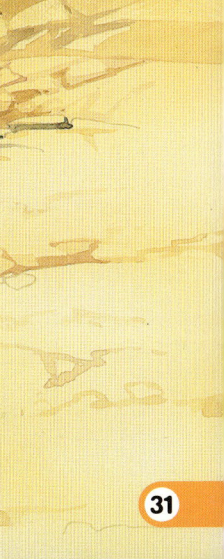

April 1923

It's almost one year later, and I have been bitten by the dinosaur bug again. When I brought the skeleton of *Baluchitherium* back to the musuem, the discovery sent shock waves through the establishment, and it has brought me worldwide fame. Henry Fairfield Osborn described it as one of the greatest dinosaur finds ever. I know this is just the tip of the iceberg and there's more to be found in those shifting sands. So our convoy has taken to the road once again, leaving behind the safety of the city of Peking to steer into the Gobi.

June 1923

Yet again, I am proved right! Yesterday, one of my assistants, George Olson, came back to the camp with news of an incredible discovery: a dinosaur nest. We returned with him to an area known as the Flaming Cliffs. There I saw three eggs sticking up out of the rock. Each was the size of a soccer ball. At long last, we have proof that dinosaurs laid eggs and did not give birth to live young. We investigated further and found the skeleton of a small dinosaur on top of the nest. It's possible that this was a nest robber, trying to steal the eggs to eat.

July 1923

The hunt continues, but we have had a setback. I have been ambushed! Today, while I was scouting ahead of the rest of the team in one of the cars, three strange men appeared on horseback. The bandits drew their rifles, but before they could shoot, I drove toward them at full speed, firing my revolver. The horses bucked wildly, and the bandits fled. It was a lucky escape. Mongolia is a wild place. We need to take a break.

June 1925

A couple of years later, and the expedition is on again. We have set up camp on a desert ridge. I am certain the area is a treasure trove of fossils. However, there is a big problem – the rocks are crawling with poisonous snakes. It's a relief to return to the safety of our camp each night.

July 1925

Disaster has struck! We have been attacked by the snakes. Last night was bitterly cold, and we awoke to find the camp overrun. The snakes had been searching for a warm place to spend the night. They slithered into our tents, crawled over the beds and even wriggled under the blankets!

We panicked and ran screaming. Finally, when we came to our senses, we started to drive the snakes away. We must have killed at least fifty of them, but they just kept coming back. The struggle continued all night. It's a miracle none of us died, although my poor dog was bitten and is badly shaken. Since yesterday, I have been thinking long and hard about this trip. I've decided it's too dangerous for us to remain. Too many lives are at risk. We must pack up our discoveries and go home. Will we ever return?

A Tale to Tell

Roy Chapman Andrews and his team did return to Asia and continued their thrilling adventures for another four years. They were machine-gunned by Chinese troops, and accused of spying by the Russian government. Finally, in 1930, Chapman accepted that it really was too risky to carry on. He returned to America with his crates of fossils and took a job at the museum. By now, he was the most famous dinosaur hunter in the world. He spent the rest of his life writing books about his adventures. These books inspired a whole generation of young archaeologists.

Letter Ladder

Use the clues below to fill in the boxes. If you've answered correctly, the shaded squares will spell out a type of dinosaur.

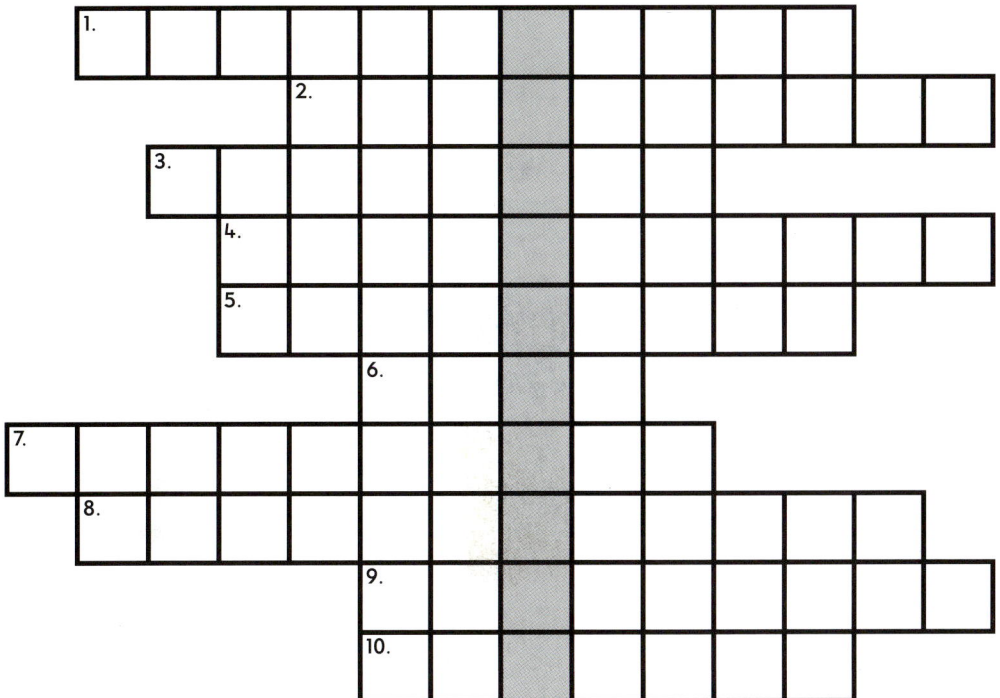

1. Plant-eating dinosaur with three horns and a bony neck frill.
2. One of the largest dinosaurs, with an extremely long neck.
3. Flowering plant from Cretaceous times.
4. Four-legged dinosaur with plates on its back and spikes on its tail.
5. Dinosaur that nested in large groups and looked after its babies.
6. *Deinonychus* had a huge one of these on each back foot.
7. Flying reptiles that lived during the time of the dinosaurs.
8. Small, meat-eating dinosaur whose name means "swift thief."
9. Dinosaur that picked plants by hand, then ground them up with blunt teeth.
10. The name for dinosaur remains such as bones or teeth.

True or False?

Which of these facts are true and which are false?
If you have read this book carefully, you will know the answers!

1 The dinosaurs lived during a time called the Mesozoic era.

2 *Baryonyx* caught fish with the huge hook on its head.

3 *Sinosauropteryx* had a feather-like covering on its skin.

4 Dinosaurs gave birth to their young by laying eggs.

5 Ichthyosaurs were flying reptiles that lived alongside the dinosaurs.

6 The dinosaurs died out about five million years ago.

7 *Compsognathus* was one of the largest dinosaurs.

8 A person who studies fossils is called a palaeontologist.

9 All dinosaurs were carnivores and only ever ate meat.

10 The word dinosaur means "terrible lizard."

11 It was much warmer during the time of the dinosaurs than it is now.

12 When the dinosaurs roamed the Earth, no mammals were living.

ANSWERS: 1. True 2. False 3. True 4. True 5. False 6. False 7. False 8. True 9. False 10. True 11. True 12. False

Dino Word Search

See if you can solve this dinosaur word search. All of the words
listed below can be found by reading either forward,
backward, or diagonally. When you find a word,
circle it on the grid and cross it off the list.

A	C	T	R	A	C	K	W	A	Y	S	B
J	L	A	S	I	E	C	J	P	T	V	X
U	A	W	R	E	P	T	I	L	E	Z	C
R	W	M	L	N	F	K	A	Q	U	S	E
A	S	R	J	Y	I	A	H	I	K	P	R
S	A	D	M	A	G	V	B	F	L	I	O
S	U	F	T	A	W	Q	O	T	C	K	T
I	R	T	P	S	M	S	N	R	R	E	A
C	O	E	G	G	S	M	H	W	E	S	D
L	P	E	V	I	D	E	A	X	S	N	E
G	O	T	L	M	U	B	Z	L	T	D	R
H	D	H	O	R	N	S	F	Y	O	C	P

fossil	teeth	reptile	horns
Jurassic	carnivore	trackways	crest
predator	tail	claws	mammal
eggs	sauropod	spikes	jaws

Glossary

amphibian: an animal that can live in and out of water, such as a frog or a toad. During the time of the dinosaurs, there were amphibians the size of pigs.

carnivore: an animal that eats meat

conifer: a tree with needle-shaped leaves that produces seeds in cones. Conifers were plentiful in Triassic and Jurassic times.

continent: a huge area of land that is surrounded by ocean. There are seven continents in the world today. When the dinosaurs first appeared, there was one giant continent called Pangaea.

Cretaceous period: the time in the Earth's history that lasted from 145 to 65 million years ago. At the end of the Cretaceous period, the dinosaurs died out.

evolve: to develop or change slowly over millions of years. Dinosaurs evolved, or developed gradually, over a long period of time. They slowly adapted to suit their environment.

fossil: the remains of an animal or plant that died millions of years ago. Fossils are left behind in rocks and minerals. They can include bones, teeth, and footprints.

herbivore: an animal that eats plants

Jurassic period: the time in Earth's history that lasted from 205 to 145 million years ago

mammal: a warm-blooded animal with hair or fur that gives birth to live young and feeds its babies on milk from its body

Mesozoic era: the time in Earth's history from 250 to 65 million years ago. It is divided into the Triassic, Jurassic, and Cretaceous periods.

meteorite: a rock from space that has hit the Earth

ornithischian: the name given to a dinosaur with hip bones shaped like those of birds. *Stegosaurus* and *Iguanadon* are examples of bird-hipped dinosaurs.

paleontologist: a scientist who studies and dates fossils to find out about the history of life

poles: the farthest points north and south on the earth. Today the earth's poles are covered with ice. During the time of the dinosaurs, there was no ice at the poles.

predator: an animal that hunts and kills other animals for food

prey: an animal that is hunted and eaten by other animals

reptile: a cold-blooded animal, such as a lizard, with scaly skin. Most reptiles give birth to their young by laying eggs.

saurischian: the name given to a dinosaur with hip bones shaped like those of lizards. *Tyrannosaurus* and *Diplodocus* are examples of lizard-hipped dinosaurs.

sauropod: any large, plant-eating dinosaur with a long neck, such as *Diplodocus*

theropod: any two-legged, meat-eating dinosaur, such as *Tyrannosaurus*

Triassic period: the time in Earth's history from 250 to 205 million years ago

Dinosaur Pronounciation

Use this pronunciation guide to say the names of the dinosaurs and other ancient animals in this book correctly.

Albertosaurus (al-BERT-oh-SAW-rus)

Allosaurus (al-oh-SAW-rus)

Alphadon (AL-fa-don)

Ankylosaurus (an-KY-loh-SAW-rus)

Archaeopteryx (AR-kee-OP-te-riks)

Argentinosaurus (ar-gen-TIN-oh-SAW-rus)

Apatosaurus (a-PAT-oh-SAW-rus)

Baryonyx (ba-ree-O-niks)

Brachiosaurus (BRAK-ee-oh-SAW-rus)

Compsognathus (COMP-sog-NAY-thus)

Corythosaurus (KOR-ee-thoh-SAW-rus)

Deinonychus (dy-non-I-kus)

Diplodocus (dip-LOD-oh-kus)

Eoraptor (EE-oh-RAP-tor)

Euoplocephalus (YOO-oh-plo-SEF-al-us)

Gallimimus (GAL-ee-MIME-us)

Ichthyosaur (IK-thee-oh-sawr)

Iguanodon (ig-WAAN-oh-don)

Maiasaura (MY-a-SAW-ra)

Minmi (MIN-mee)

Nodosaurus (NOD-oh-SAW-rus)

Ornithomimus (or-NITH-oh-MIME-us)

Parasaurolophus (PAR-a-SAW-roh-LOAF-us)

Plateosaurus (plat-ee-oh-SAW-rus)

Plesiosaur (PLEE-zee-oh-sawr)

Protoceratops (PRO-toe-SER-a-tops)

Pterosaur (TER-oh-sawr)

Sauroposeidon (SAW-roh-pos-EYE-don)

Sinosauropteryx (SIGN-oh-sawr-OP-te-riks)

Stegosaurus (STEG-oh-SAW-rus)

Struthiomimus (STROOTH-ee-oh-MIME-us)

Tenontosaurus (ten-ON-toh-SAW-rus)

Triceratops (try-SER-a-tops)

Tyrannosaurus (ty-RAN-oh-SAW-rus)

Velociraptor (vel-OSS-i-rap-tor)

Your INTERFACT CD-ROM will run on both PCs with Windows and on Apple Macs. To make sure that your computer meets the system requirements, check the list below.

MINIMUM SYSTEM REQUIREMENTS

PC

Processor: Pentium II (266 MHz) or higher

Windows 95, 98, ME, 2000, or XP

Monitor: SVGA color monitor

Screen resolution: 640 x 480 pixels x 24-bit Color

Graphics card: 4MB or above

Soundcard: SoundBlaster compatible

Memory: 32MB of RAM

Headphones or speakers

CD-ROM drive: four-speed or greater

APPLE MACINTOSH

Processor: 200 MHz Power Mac, G3 or iMac

Operating system 8.1–9.x

Monitor: Millions of Colors

Screen resolution: 640 x 480 pixels

Graphics card: 4MB or above

Soundcard: SoundBlaster compatible

Memory: 32MB of RAM

Headphones or speakers

CD-ROM drive: four-speed or greater

Loading Your INTERFACT Disk

INTERFACT is easy to load. You can run INTERFACT from the CD-ROM – you don't need to install it on your hard drive. But, before you begin, quickly run through the checklist below to ensure that your computer is ready to run the program.

PC WITH WINDOWS

The program should start automatically when you put the disk in the CD-ROM drive. If it does not, follow these instructions.

❶ Put the disk in the CD-ROM drive

❷ Double-click on MY COMPUTER

❸ Double-click on CD-ROM drive icon

❹ Double-click on the DINOSAURS icon

APPLE MACINTOSH

❶ Put the disk in the CD-ROM drive

❷ Double-click on the INTERFACT icon

❸ Double-click on the DINOSAURS icon

CHECKLIST

● First, make sure that your computer and monitor meet the system requirements listed on page 40.

● Ensure that your computer, monitor, and CD-ROM drive are all switched on and working normally.

● It is important that you do not have any other applications, such as word processors, running. Before starting INTERFACT, quit all other applications.

● Make sure that any screen savers for your computer have been switched off.

How to Use INTERFACT

INTERFACT is easy to use.
Now that you know how to load the
program (see page 41), read these simple
instructions and dive in!

There are five different exciting games to play. Use the controls on the right-hand side of the screen to select the one you want to try. You will see that the main area of the screen changes as you click on to different games.

For example, this is what your screen will look like when you play DINOS IN DISGUISE, a game where you use clues to work out which dinosaur is hiding in the cave. When you've selected a game, click on the main screen to start playing. Have fun!

Click here to select the game you want to play.

Click on the arrow keys to scroll through the different games on the disk or to find your way to the exit.

Click on the speaker button to hear the text read aloud.

Main Screen

DISK LINKS

When you read the book, you'll come across Disk Links. These icons show you where to find activities on the disk that relate to the page you are reading. Use the arrow keys to find the icon on screen that matches the one in the Disk Link.

DISK LINK

Listen to the clues to bring the mystery dinosaur out of the cave when you play DINOS IN DISGUISE.

BOOKMARKS

As you play the games on the disk, you'll bump into Bookmarks. These icons show you where to look in the book for more information about the topic on screen. Just turn to the page of the book shown in the Bookmark.

23

ACTIVITIES

Look for the activities on pages 35 to 37 of this book. You'll find a true-or-false quiz, a dinosaur word search, and a tricky letter ladder to try.

HOT DISK TIPS

● If you need help finding your way around the disk, click the arrow keys to bring up the HELP icon, then click on the HELP icon to go to the HELP section.

Help icon

left arrow

right arrow

● Any words that appear on screen in a different color and underlined are "hot." This means that you can touch them with the cursor for more information or an explanation of the word.

● Keep a close eye on the cursor. When it changes from an arrow ↑ to a hand ☝, click your mouse and something will happen!

● After you have selected a game, move your cursor to the main screen, then click. You are now ready to play.

Troubleshooting

If you have a problem with your INTERFACT disk, you should find the solution here. If you still have a problem, then send us an e-mail at helpline@two-canpublishing.com.

Your Computer Setup

RESETTING SCREEN RESOLUTION

Resetting screen resolution in Windows 95, 98, Me, 2000, or XP:
Click on START at the bottom left of your screen, then click on SETTINGS, then CONTROL PANEL, then double-click on DISPLAY. Click on the SETTINGS tab at the top. Reset the Desktop area (or Display area) to 640 x 480 pixels and choose 24-bit Color, then click APPLY. You may then need to restart your computer.

Resetting screen resolution for Apple Macintosh:
Click on the Apple symbol at the top left of your screen to access APPLE MENU ITEMS. Select CONTROL PANELS, then MONITORS (or MONITORS AND SOUND), set the resolution to 640 x 480, and choose MILLIONS OF COLORS. Close the Monitors dialog box.

Screen resolutions can also be reset by clicking on the checkerboard symbol on the Control Strip.

ADJUSTING VIRTUAL MEMORY

Adjusting the Virtual Memory in Windows 95, 98, Me, 2000, or XP:
We do not recommend adjusting these settings. Windows will automatically configure your system as required.

Adjusting the Virtual Memory on Apple Macintosh:
If you have 32 MB of RAM or more, DINOSAURS will run faster. If you do not have this amount of RAM free, hard disk memory can be used by switching on Virtual Memory. Select the APPLE MENU, CONTROL PANELS, then MEMORY. Switch on Virtual Memory. Set the amount of memory you require, then restart your machine.

Common Problems

Disk will not run
There is not enough memory available. Quit all other applications and programs. If this does not work, increase your machine's RAM by adjusting the Virtual Memory (see left).

There is no sound
(Try each of the following)

1 Ensure that your speakers or headphones are connected to the speaker outlet at the back of your computer. Make sure they are not plugged into the audio socket next to the CD-ROM drive at the front of the computer.

2 Ensure that the volume control is turned up (on your external speakers and by using internal volume control).

3 (PCs only) Your sound card is not SoundBlaster compatible. To make your settings SoundBlaster compatible, see your sound card manual for more information.

Graphics do not load or are of poor quality
Not enough memory is available or you have the wrong display setting. Quit other applications and make sure that your screen resolution is set to 640 x 480 pixels with 24-bit Color.

Graphics freeze or text boxes appear blank (Windows 95 or 98 only)
Graphics card acceleration is too high. Right-click your mouse on MY COMPUTER. Click on PROPERTIES, then PERFORMANCE, then GRAPHICS. Reset the hardware acceleration slider to "None." Click OK. Restart your computer.

Your machine freezes
There is not enough memory available. Either quit other applications and programs or increase your machine's RAM by adjusting the Virtual Memory (see left).

If you continue to have problems, check the ReadMe file on your Interfact disk for more information or contact your computer supplier.

45

Index

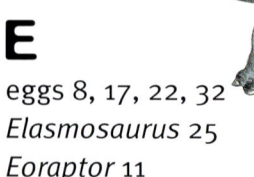

CHECK OUT THE INTERFACT SERIES

There is a huge range of INTERFACT titles to choose from, covering science, history, and nature topics.

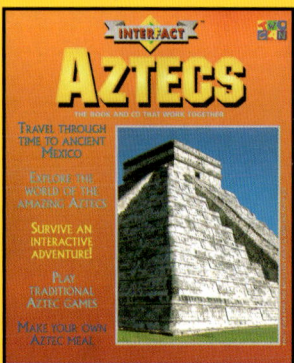

ISBN 1-58728-450-2

History

Ancient Greece
1-58728-455-3
Aztecs
1-58728-450-2
Egyptians
1-58728-458-8
Romans
1-58728-462-6
Vikings
1-58728-467-7

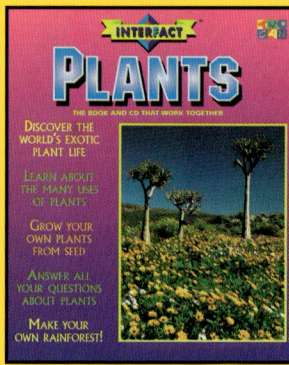

ISBN 1-58728-460-X

Animals & Nature

Coral Reefs
1-58728-456-1
Deserts
1-58728-457-X
Dinosaurs
1-58728-343-3
Oceans
1-58728-459-6
Plants
1-58728-460-X
Polar Lands
1-58728-452-9
Rainforests
1-58728-461-8
Sharks
1-58728-344-1
Storms
1-58728-466-9
Volcanoes
1-58728-468-5

ISBN 1-58728-465-0

Science

Air
1-58728-454-5
Electricity & Magnetism
1-58728-451-0
Senses
1-58728-463-4
Solar System
1-58728-464-2
Space Travel
1-58728-465-0
Water
1-58728-469-3
Weather
1-58728-470-7

ISBN 1-58728-461-8

For all orders or for more information, please contact Two-Can Publishing, 18705 Lake Drive East, Chanhassen, MN 55317 • Tel: 1-800-328-3895
Fax: 952-932-0386 • email: helpline@two-canpublishing.com
Please visit our website: www.two-canpublishing.com

TWOCAN ™